FROM THE HILLS OF DREAM

THRENODIES, SONGS AND OTHER POEMS

WILLIAM SHARP

Published by Left of Brain Books

Copyright © 2021 Left of Brain Books

ISBN 978-1-396-32240-2

First Edition

All rights reserved. No part of this publication may be reproduced, distributed, or transmitted in any form or by any means, including photocopying, recording, or other electronic or mechanical methods, without the prior written permission of the publisher, except in the case of brief quotations embodied in critical reviews and certain other noncommercial uses permitted by copyright law. Left of Brain Books is a division of Left of Brain Onboarding Pty Ltd.

Table of Contents

THROUGH THE IVORY GATE

UNDER THE EVENING STAR	1
THE ENCHANTED VALLEYS	1
THE VALLEY OF WHITE POPPIES	2
THE VALLEY OF SILENCE	2
DREAM MEADOWS	3
GREY PASTURES	4
LONGING	4
REMEMBRANCE	4
THE SINGER IN THE WOODS	5
REQUIEM	6

FROM THE HEART OF A WOMAN

I

THE PRAYER OF WOMEN	7
THE RUNE OF THE SORROW OF WOMEN	9
THE RUNE OF THE PASSION OF WOMAN	11
THE SHEPHERD	14

II

WHITE STAR OF TIME	16
GREEN BRANCHES	16
SHULE, SHULE, SHULE, AGRAH!	16
LORD OF MY LIFE	17
ISLA	18
AN IMMORTAL	19
THE VISION	19
HUSHING SONG	20

Mo-Lennav-a-Chree	21
Lullaby	21
My Birdeen	22
Pulse of my Heart	23
The Rose of Flame	24
The Undersong	24
The Lonely Hunter	25
The White Peace	26

FROM THE HILLS OF DREAM

From the Hills of Dream	27
The Unknown Wind	28
Little Children of the Wind	28
A Milking Sian	28
The Kye-song of St. Bride	29
St. Bride's Lullaby	30
When the Dew is Falling	31
Invocation of Peace	32
In the Silences of the Woods	33
Mater Consolatrix	33
The Soul's Armageddon	33
Cantilena Mundi	34
The Hills of Ruel	35
The Bugles of Dreamland	36
Dalua	37
The Lords of Shadow	38
Morag of the Glen	38
The Moon-Child	39
The Rune of the Four Winds	40

Naoi Miannain	41
Nine Desires	42

FOAM OF THE PAST
THRENODIES AND SONGS CHANTS AND DIRGES

To W. B. Yeats	43
White-Hands	46
Heart O' Beauty	46
Oona of the Dark Eyes and the Crying of Wind	47
The Lament of Ian the Proud	48
The Monody of Isla the Singer	48
The End of Aodh-of-the-Songs	49
The Love-chant of Cormac Conlingas	50
The Washer of the Ford	50
The Death-Dirge for Cathal	51
The Moon-Song of Cathal	52
The Sun-Chant Of Cathal	53
The Song of Fionula	53
The Chant of Ardan the Pict	54
The Song of Deirdrê	55
The Death Shadow	56
The Meditation of Colum	57
The Lamentation of Balva the Monk	58
The Last Night of Artân the Culdee	58
The Death Dance	59
The Song of Ahez the Pale	60

CLOSING DOORS

Closing Doors	61
The Star of Beauty	61

In the Shadow	62
The Cup	63
An Old Tale of Three	63
The Crimson Moon	64
The Tryst of Queen Hynde	65
The Love-Kiss of Dermid and Grainne	67
The Song of Fionula	68
Dim Face of Beauty	68
The Mourners	69
Dead Love	70
The Rune of Age	70
Leaves, Shadows, and Dreams	71
The Voice Among the Dunes	72
The Veiled Avenger	72
The Three Evils of the Night	74
The Burthen of the Tide	75
The Bells of Sorrow	75
Miann	76
Desires	76

TO A MEMORY

THE HILLS OF DREAM
St. John's Eve 1901

THERE *has been twilight here, since one whom some name Life and some Death slid between us the little shadow that is the unfathomable dark and silence. In a grave deeper than is hollowed under the windsweet grass lies that which was so passing fair.*

Who plays the Song of Songs upon the Hills of Dream? It is said Love is that reed-player, for there is no song like his.

But to-day I saw one, on these dim garths of shadow and silence, who put a reed to his lips and played a white spell of beauty. Then I knew Love and Death to be one, as in the old myth of Oengus of the White Birds and the Grey Shadows.

Here are the broken airs that once you loved....

> *"The fable-flowering land wherein they grew*
> *Hath dreams for stars, and grey romance for dew."*

They are but the breath of what has been: only are they for this, that they do the will of beauty and regret.

Green thou would'st not be plucked, thy purple fruit I longed for....
                                    THE STEPHANOS OF PHILIPPUS.

*Là-bas, tout nous appelle.... Et, qui sait, tous les rêves à réalizer!...
A quoi bon les réalizer... ils sont si beaux!*
                                                                    AXEL.

Love is as a vapour that is licked up of the wind. Let whoso longeth after this lovely mist—that as a breath is, and is not—beware of this wind. There is no sorrow like unto the sorrow of this wind.
                            LEABHRAN MHÒR-GHEASADAIREACHD.
                                    (The Little Book of the Great Enchantment)

"The waves of the sea have spoken to me; the wild birds have taught me; the music of many waters has been my master."
                                                                KALEVALA.

THROUGH THE IVORY GATE

Under the Evening Star

POOR little songs, children of sorrow, go.
A wind may take you up, and blow you far.
My heart will go with you, too, wherever you go.

As the little leaves in the wood they pass:
The wind has lifted them, and the wind is gone.
Have I too not heard the wind come, and pass?

The secret dews fall under the Evening-Star,
And there is peace I know in the west: yet, if there be no dawn,
The secret dews fall under the Evening-Star.

The Enchanted Valleys

BY the Gate of Sleep we enter the Enchanted Valleys.
White soundless birds fly near the twilit portals:
Follow, and they lead to the Silent Alleys.

Grey pastures are there, and hush'd spell-bound woods,
And still waters, girt with unwhispering reeds:
Lost dreams linger there, wan multitudes:

They haunt the grey waters, the alleys dense and dim,
The immemorial woods of timeless age,
And where the forest leans on the grey sea's rim.

Nothing is there of gladness or of sorrow:
What is past can neither be glad nor sad:
It is past: there is no dawn: no to-morrow.

The Valley of White Poppies

BETWEEN the grey pastures and the dark wood
A valley of white poppies is lit by the low moon:
   It is the grave of dreams, a holy rood.

   It is quiet there: no wind doth ever fall.
Long long ago a wind sang once a heart-sweet rune.
   Now the white poppies grow, silent and tall.

   A white bird floats there like a drifting leaf:
It feeds upon faint sweet hopes and perishing dreams
   And the still breath of unremembering grief.

   And as a silent leaf the white bird passes,
Winnowing the dusk by dim forgetful streams.
   I am alone now among the silent grasses.

The Valley of Silence

   IN the secret Valley of Silence
      No breath doth fall;
   No wind stirs in the branches;
      No bird doth call:
      As on a white wall
         A breathless lizard is still,
      So silence lies on the valley
         Breathlessly still.

In the dusk-grown heart of the valley
      An altar rises white:
No rapt priest bends in awe
      Before its silent light:
      But sometimes a flight
         Of breathless words of prayer
      White-wing'd enclose the altar,
         Eddies of prayer.

Dream Meadows

GIRT with great garths of shadow
    Dim meadows fade in grey:
No moon lightens the gloaming,
    The meadows know no day:
        But pale shapes shifting
        From dusk to dusk, or lifting
        Frail wings in flight, go drifting
    Adown each flowerless way.

These phantom-dreams in shadow
    Were once in wild-rose flame;
Each wore a star of glory,
    Each had a loved sweet name:
        Now they are nameless, knowing
        Nor star nor flame, but going
        Whither they know not, flowing
    Waves without wind or aim.

But later through the gloaming
    The Midnight-Shepherd cries:
The trooping shadows follow
    Making a wind of sighs:
        The fold is hollow and black;
        No pathway thence, no track;
        No dream ever comes back
    Beneath those silent skies.

GREY PASTURES

    IN the grey gloaming where the white moth flies—
When I, quiet dust on the forgetful wind,
    Shall be untroubled by any breath of sighs—

    It may be I shall fall like dew upon
The still breath of grey pastures such as these
    Wherein I wander now twixt dusk and dawn.

    See, in this phantom bloom I leave a kiss:
It was given me in fire; now it is grey dust:
    Mayhap I may thrill again at the touch of this.

LONGING

O WOULD I were the cool wind that's blowing from the sea,
Each loneliest valley I would search till I should come to thee.

In the dew on the grass is your name, dear, i' the leaf on the tree—
O would I were the cool wind that's blowing from the sea.

O would I were the cool wind that's blowing far from me—
The grey silence, the grey waves, the grey wastes of the sea.

REMEMBRANCE

    NO more: let there be no more said.
It is over now, the long hope, the beautiful dream.
    The poor body of love in his grave is laid.

    I had dreamed his shining eyes eternal, alas!
Now, dead love, I know, can never rise again.
    Never, never again shall I see even his shadow pass.

A star has ceased to shine in my lonely skies.
Sometimes I dream I see it shining in my heart,
    As a bird the windless pool over which it flies.

No: no more: I will not say what I see, there:
Sorrow has depths within depths . . . silence is best:
    Farewell, Dead Love: no more the same road we fare.

The Singer in the Woods

"Where Memory but a voice. . . ."

WHERE moongrey-thistled dunes divide the woods from the sea
Sometimes a phantom drifts like smoke from tree to tree:
His voice is as the thin faint song when the wind wearily
Sighs in the grass, and sighing dies: barely it comes to me.

Sometimes I hear the sighing voice along the shadowy shore;
Sometimes wave-borne it comes, as when on labouring oar
Dying men sigh once, and die, at the closing of the door
They hear below the muffled tides or the dull drowning roar.

Sometimes he passes through the caves where twilight dies:
His voice like mist from a valley then doth rise,
Or in a windy flight of gathered sighs
Is blown like perishing smoke against the midnight skies.

But oftenest in the dark woods I hear him sing
Dim, half remembered things where the old mosses cling
To the old trees, and the faint wandering eddies bring
The phantom echoes of a phantom Spring.

Lost in the dark gulf of the woods, his song sinks low:
I listen: and hear only the long, inevitable, slow
Falling of wave on wave, the sighing flow:
And in the silence my heart sobbing its old woe.

REQUIEM

IN the sunken city of Murias
    A golden Image dwells:
The sea-song of the trampling waves
    Is as muffled bells
    Where He dwells
In the city of Murias.

In the sunken city of Murias
    A golden Image gleams:
The loud noise of the moving seas
    Is as woven beams,
    Where He dreams
In the city of Murias.

In the sunken city of Murias,
    Deep, deep beneath the sea
The Image sits and hears Time break
    The heart I gave to thee
    And thou to me,
In the city of Murias.

In the sunken city of Murias
    Long, oh so long ago
Our souls were wed when the world young:
    Are we old now, that we know
    This silent woe
In the City of Murias?

In the sunken city of Murias
    A graven Image dwells:
The sound of our little sobbing prayer
    Is as muffled bells
    Where He dwells
In the city of Murias.

FROM THE HEART OF A WOMAN

"The great winding sheets that bury all things in oblivion, are two: Love, that makes oblivious of Life; and Death, that obliterates Love."

"Was it because I desired thee darkly, that thou could'st not know the white spell? Or was it that the white spell could not reach thy darkness? One god debateth this: and another god answereth this: but one god knoweth it. With him be the issue."

AN LEABHAR BÀN.
(The Book of White Magic.)

"My wisdom became pregnant on lonely mountains; upon rugged stones she bore her young.
Now she runneth strangely through the bard desert and seeketh, and ever seeketh for soft grass, mine own old wisdom."

NIETZSCHE.

I

The Prayer of Women

O SPIRIT that broods upon the hills
And moves upon the face of the deep,
And is heard in the wind,
Save us from the desire of men's eyes,
And the cruel lust of them.
Save us from the springing of the cruel seed
In that narrow house which is as the grave
For darkness and loneliness . . .
That women carry with them with shame, and
    weariness, and long pain,
Only for the laughter of man's heart,
And for the joy that triumphs therein,
And the sport that is in his heart,

Wherewith he mocketh us,
Wherewith he playeth with us,
Wherewith he trampleth upon us . . .
Us, who conceive and bear him;
Us, who bring him forth;
Who feed him in the womb, and at the breast, and at
    the knee:
Whom he calleth mother and wife,
And mother again of his children and his children's
    children.
Ah, hour of the hours,
When he looks at our hair and sees it is grey;
And at our eyes and sees they are dim;
And at our lips straightened out with long pain;
And at our breasts, fallen and seared as a barren hill;
And at our hands, worn with toil!
Ah, hour of the hours,
When, seeing, he seeth all the bitter ruin and wreck
    of us—
All save the violated womb that curses him—
All save the heart that forbeareth . . . for pity—
All save the living brain that condemneth him—
All save the spirit that shall not mate with him—
All save the soul he shall never see
Till he be one with it, and equal;
He who hath the bridal, but guideth not;
He who hath the whip, yet is driven;
He who as a shepherd calleth upon us,
But is himself a lost sheep, crying among the hills!
O Spirit, and the Nine Angels who watch us,
And Thou, white Christ, and Mary Mother of
    Sorrow,
Heal us of the wrong of man:
We whose breasts are weary with milk,
Cry, cry to Thee, O Compassionate!

The Rune of the Sorrow of Women

This is the rune of the women who bear in sorrow;
Who, having anguish of body, die in the pangs of bearing,
Who, with the ebb at the heart, pass ere the wane of the babe-month.

THE RUNE

O WE are tired, we are tired, all we who are women:
Heavy the breasts with milk that never shall nourish:
Heavy the womb that never again shall be weighty.
For we have the burthen upon us, we have the burthen,
The long slow pain, and the sorrow of going, and the parting.
O little hands, O little lips, farewell and farewell.
Bitter the sorrow of bearing only to end with the parting.

THE DREAM

Far away in the east of the world a Woman had sorrow.
Heavy she was with child, and the pains were upon her.
Then God looked forth out of heaven, and he spake in his pity:
"O Mary, thou bearest the Prince of Peace, and thy seed shall be
    blessëd."
But Mary the Mother sighed, and God the All-Seeing wondered,
For this is the rune he heard in the heart of Mary the Virgin:—
"Man blindfold soweth the seed, and blindly he reapeth:
And lo the word of the Lord is a blessing upon the sower.
O what of the blessing upon the field that is sown,
What of the sown, not the sower, what of the mother, the bearer?
Sure it is this that I see: that everywhere over the world
The man has the pain and the sorrow, the weary womb and the
    travail!
Everywhere patient he is, restraining the tears of his patience,
Slow in upbraiding, swift in passion unselfish,
Bearing his pain in silence, in silence the shame and the anguish:
Slow, slow he is to put the blame on the love of the woman:

Slow to say that she led him astray, swift ever to love and excuse her!
O 'tis a good thing, and glad I am at the seeing,
That man who has all the pain and the patient sorrow and waiting
Keepeth his heart ever young and never upbraideth the woman
For that she laughs in the sun and taketh the joy of her living
And holdeth him to her breast, and knoweth pleasure,
And plighteth troth akin to the starry immortals,
And soon forgetteth, and lusteth after another,
And plighteth again, and again, and yet again and again,
And asketh one thing only of man who is patient and loving,—
This: that he swerve not ever, that faithful he be and loyal,
And know that the sorrow of sorrows is only a law of his being,
And all is well with woman, and the world of woman, and God.
O 'tis a good thing, and glad I am at the seeing!
And this is the rune of man the bearer of pain and sorrow,
The father who giveth the babe his youth, his joy and the life of his
    living!"—

(And high in His Heaven God the All-Seeing troubled.)

THE RUNE

O we are weary, how weary, all we of the burthen:
Heavy the breasts with milk that never shall nourish:
Heavy the womb that never again shall be fruitful:
Heavy the hearts that never again shall be weighty.
For we have the burthen upon us, we have the burthen,
The long slow pain, and the sorrow of going, and the parting.
O little hands, O little lips, farewell and farewell:
Bitter the sorrow of bearing only to end with the parting,
Bitter the sorrow of bearing only to end with the parting.

The Rune of the Passion of Woman

WE who love are those who suffer,
We who suffer most are those who most do love.
O the heartbreak come of longing love,
O the heartbreak come of love deferred,
O the heartbreak come of love grown listless.
Far upon the lonely hills I have heard the crying,
The lamentable crying of the ewes,
And dreamed I heard the sorrow of poor mothers
Made lambless too and weary with that sorrow:
And far upon the waves I have heard the crying,
The lamentable crying of the seamews,
And dreamed I heard the wailing of the women
Whose hearts are flamed with love above the grave-stone,
Whose hearts beat fast but hear no fellow-beating.
Bitter, alas, the sorrow of lonely women,
When no man by the ingle sits, and in the cradle
No little flower-like faces flush with slumber:
Bitter the loss of these, the lonely silence,
The void bed, the hearthside void,
The void heart, and only the grave not void:
But bitterer, oh more bitter still, the longing
Of women who have known no love at all, who never,
Never, never, have grown hot and cold with rapture
'Neath the lips or 'neath the clasp of longing,
Who have never opened eyes of heaven to man's devotion,
Who have never heard a husband whisper "wife,"
Who have lost their youth, their dreams, their fairness,
In a vain upgrowing to a light that comes not.
Bitter these: but bitterer than either,
O most bitter for the heart of woman
To have loved and been beloved with passion,
To have known the height and depth, the vision
Of triple-flaming love—and in the heart-self

Sung a song of deathless love, immortal,
Sunrise-haired, and starry-eyed, and wondrous:
To have felt the brain sustain the mighty
Weight and reach of thought unspanned and spanless,
To have felt the soul grow large and noble,
To have felt the spirit dauntless, eager, swift in hope and
    daring,
To have felt the body grow in fairness,
All the glory and the beauty of the body
Thrill with joy of living, feel the bosom
Rise and fall with sudden tides of passion,
Feel the lift of soul to soul, and know the rapture
Of the rising triumph of the ultimate dream
Beyond the pale place of defeated dreams:
To know all this, to feel all this, to be a woman
Crowned with the double crown of lily and rose
And have the morning star to rule the golden hours
And have the evening star thro' hours of dream,
To live, to do, to act, to dream, to hope,
To be a perfect woman with the full
Sweet, wondrous, and consummate joy
Of womanhood fulfilled to all desire—
And then . . . oh then, to know the waning of the vision,
To go through days and nights of starless longing,
Through nights and days of gloom and bitter sorrow:
To see the fairness of the body passing,
To see the beauty wither, the sweet colour
Fade, the coming of the wintry lines
Upon pale faces chilled with idle loving,
The slow subsidence of the tides of living.
To feel all this, and know the desolate sorrow
Of the pale place of all defeated dreams,
And to cry out with aching lips, and vainly;
And to cry out with aching heart, and vainly;
And to cry out with aching brain, and vainly;

And to cry out with aching soul, and vainly;
To cry, cry, cry with passionate heartbreak, sobbing,
To the dim wondrous shape of Love Retreating—
To grope blindly for the warm hand, for the swift touch,
To seek blindly for the starry lamps of passion,
To crave blindly for the dear words of longing!
To go forth cold, and drear, and lonely, O so lonely,
With the heart-cry even as the crying,
The lamentable crying on the hills
When lambless ewes go desolately astray—
Yea, to go forth discrowned at last, who have worn
The flower-sweet lovely crown of rapturous love:
To know the eyes have lost their starry wonder;
To know the hair no more a fragrant dusk
Wherein to whisper secrets of deep longing;
To know the breasts shall henceforth be no haven
For the dear weary head that loved to lie there—
To go, to know, and yet to live and suffer,
To be as use and wont demand, to fly no signal
That the soul founders in a sea of sorrow,
But to be 'true,' 'a woman,' 'patient,' 'tender,'
'Divinely acquiescent,' all-forbearing,
To laugh, and smile, to comfort, to sustain,
To do all this—oh this is bitterest,
O this the heaviest cross, O this the tree
Whereon the woman hath her crucifixion.

But O ye women, what avail? Behold,
Men worship at the tree, whereon is writ
The legend of the broken hearts of women.
And this is the end: for young and old the end:
For fair and sweet, for those not sweet nor fair,
For loved, unloved, and those who once were loved,
For all the women of all this weary world
Of joy too brief and sorrow far too long,

This is the end: the cross, the bitter tree,
And worship of the phantom raised on high
Out of your love, your passion, your despair,
Hopes unfulfilled, and unavailing tears.

The Shepherd

"Verily, those berdsmen also were of the sheep!"
NIETZSCHE.

HE loved me, as he said, in every part,
And yet I could not, would not, give him all:
Why should a woman forfeit her whole heart
At bidding of a single shepherd's call?
One vast the deep, and yet each wave is free
To answer to the noonshine's drowsy smile
Or leap to meet the storm-wind's rapturous glee:
This heart of mine a wave is oftenwhile.
Depth below depth, strange currents cross, re-cross,
The anguished eddies darkly ebb and flow,
But on the placid surface seldom toss
The reckless flotsam of what seethes below:
O placid calms and maelstrom heart of me,
Shall it be thus till there be no more sea?

II

"I am thy shepherd, love, that on this hill
Of life shall tend and guard thee evermore."
These were thy words that far-off day and still
Lives on thine echoing lips this bond of yore.
Yet who wert thou, O soul as I am, thus
To take so blithely gage of shepherding?
Were we not both astray where perilous
Steps might each into the abysmal darkness fling?
Lo, my tired soul even as a storm-stayed ewe

Across the heights unto my shepherd cried:
But to the sheltered vale at last I drew
And laid me weary by thy sleeping side.
Thou didst not hear The Shepherd calling us,
Nor far the night-wind, vibrant, ominous.

III

O shepherd of mine, lord of my little life,
Guard me from knowledge even of the stress:
And if I stray, take heed thou of thy wife,
Errant from mere womanhood's wantonness.
Even as the Lord of Hosts, lo in thy hand,
The hollow of thy hand, my soul support:
Guide this poor derelict back unto the land
And lead me, pilot, to thy sheltering port!
No—no—keep back—away—not now thy kiss:
O shepherd, pilot, wake! awake! awake!
The deep must whelm us both! Hark, the waves hiss,
And as a shaken leaf the land doth shake!
Awake, O shepherding soul, and take command!—
—Nay, vain vain words: how shall he understand?

II

WHITE STAR OF TIME

EACH love-thought in thy mind doth rise
    As some white cloud at even,
Till in sweet dews it falls on me
    Athirst for thee, my Heaven!

My Heaven, my Heaven, thou art so far!
    Stoop, since I cannot climb:
I would this wandering fire were lost
    In thee, white Star of Time!

GREEN BRANCHES

WAVE, wave, green branches, wave me far away
To where the forest deepens and the hill-winds, sleeping, stay:
Where Peace doth fold her twilight wings, and through the heart of day
There goes the rumour of passing hours grown faint and grey.

Wave, wave, green branches, my heart like a bird doth hover
Above the nesting-place your green-gloom shadows cover:
O come to my nesting heart, come close, come close, bend over,
Joy of my heart, my life, my prince, my lover!

SHULE, SHULE, SHULE, AGRAH![1]

HIS face was glad as dawn to me,
His breath was sweet as dusk to me,
His eyes were burning flames to me,
        Shule, Shule, Shule, agrah!

---

[1] I do not give the correct spelling of the Gaelic. The line signifies "Move, move, move to me, my Heart's Love."

The broad noon-day was night to me,
The full-moon night was dark to me,
The stars whirled and the poles span
The hour God took him far from me.

Perhaps he dreams in heaven now,
Perhaps he doth in worship bow,
A white flame round his foam-white brow,
      Shule, Shule, Shule, agrah!

I laugh to think of him like this,
Who once found all his joy and bliss
Against my heart, against my kiss,
      Shule, Shule, Shule, agrah!

Star of my joy, art still the same
Now thou hast gotten a new name?
Pulse of my heart, my Blood, my Flame,
      Shule, Shule, Shule, agrah!

Lord of My Life

HE laid his dear face next to mine,
His eyes aflame burned close to mine,
His heart to mine, his lips to mine,
O he was mine, all mine, all mine.

Drunk with old wine of love I was,
Drunk as the wild bee in the grass:
Yea, as the wild bee in the grass,
Drunk, drunk, with wine of love I was!

His lips of life to me were fief,
Beneath him I was but a leaf
Blown by the wind, a shaken leaf,

Yea, as the sickle reaps the sheaf,
        My Grief!
He reaped me as a gathered sheaf!

His to be gathered, his the bliss,
But not a greater bliss than this!
All of the empty world to miss
For wild redemption of his kiss!
        My Grief!

For hell was lost, though heaven was brief
Sphered in the universe of thy kiss—
So cries to thee thy fallen leaf,
Thy gathered sheaf,
Lord of my life, my Pride, my Chief,
        My Grief!

ISLA[2]

ISLA, Isla, heart of my heart, it is you alone I am loving—
    Pulse of my life, my flame, my joy, love is a bitter thing!
Love has its killing pain, they say—and you alone I am loving—
    Isla, Isla, my pride, my king, love is a bitter thing!

Isla, Isla, in the underworld where the elfin-music is,
    There we shall meet one day at last, as the wave with the wind o' the south!
Then you shall cry, "My Dream, my Queen!" and crown me with your kiss,
    And I to my kingdom come, my king, my mouth to thy mouth!

---

[2] Isla, a frequent name in the Western Highlands, is pronounced Isle-ă.

An Immortal

"For of mortal love an Immortal may be shapen."

CHILD of no mortal birth, that yet doth live,
Where loiterest thou, O blossom of our joy?
Unsummon'd hence, dost thou, knowing all, forgive
Thy rainbow-rapture, doth it never cloy?
O exquisite dream, dear child of our desire,
On mounting wings flitt'st thou afar from here?
We cannot reach thee who dost never tire,—
Sweet phantom of delight, appear, appear!
How lovely must thou be, wrought in strange fashion
From out the very breath and soul of passion . . .
With eyes as proud as his, my lover, thy sire,
When seeking through the twilight of my hair
He finds the secret flame deep hidden there,
Twin torches suddenly flashing into fire.

The Vision

    IN a fair place
        Of whin and grass,
        I heard feet pass
        Where no one was.

    I saw a face
        Bloom like a flower—
        Nay, as the rainbow-shower
        Of a tempestuous hour.

    It was not man, or woman:
    It was not human:
        But, beautiful and wild,
        Terribly undefiled,
        I knew an unborn child.

HUSHING SONG

EILY, Eily,
    My bonnie wee lass:
The winds blow,
    And the hours pass.

But never a wind
    Can do thee wrong,
Brown Birdeen, singing
    Thy bird-heart song.

And never an hour
    But has for thee
Blue of the heaven
    And green of the sea:

Blue for the hope of thee,
    Eily, Eily;
Green for the joy of thee,
    Eily, Eily.

Swing in thy nest, then,
    Here on my heart,
Birdeen, Birdeen,
    Here on my heart,
    Here on my heart!

Mo-Lennav-a-Chree

EILY, Eily, Eily, dear to me, dear and sweet,
In dreams I am hearing the sound of your little running feet—
The sound of your running feet that like the sea-hoofs beat
A music by day and night, Eily, on the sands of my heart, my Sweet!

Eily, blue i' the eyes, flower-sweet as children are,
And white as the canna that blows with the hill-breast wind afar,
Whose is the light in thine eyes—the light of a star?—a star
That sitteth supreme where the starry lights of heaven a glory are!

Eily, Eily, Eily, put off your wee hands from the heart o' me,
It is pain they are making there, where no more pain should be:
For little running feet, an' wee white hands, an' croodlin' as of the sea,
Bring tears to my eyes, Eily, tears, tears, out of the heart o' me—
Mo lennav-a-chree,
Mo lennav-a-chree!

Lullaby

LENNAVAN-MO,
Lennavan-mo,
Who is it swinging you to and fro,
With a long low swing and a sweet low croon,
And the loving words of the mother's rune?

Lennavan-mo,
Lennavan-mo,
Who is it swinging you to and fro?
I am thinking it is an angel fair,
The Angel that looks on the gulf from the lowest stair
And swings the green world upward by its leagues of sunshine hair.

Lennavan-mo,
Lennavan-mo,
Who swingeth you and the Angel to and fro?
It is He whose faintest thought is a world afar,
It is He whose wish is a leaping seven-moon'd star
It is He, Lennavan-mo,
To whom you and I and all things flow.

Lennavan-mo,
Lennavan-mo,
It is only a little wee lass you are, Eily-mo-chree,
But as this wee blossom has roots in the depths of the sky
So you are at one with the Lord of Eternity—
Bonnie wee lass that you are,
My morning-star,
Eily-mo-chree, Lennavan-mo,
    Lennavan-mo.

MY BIRDEEN

OH bonnie birdeen,
    Sweet bird of my heart—
Tell me, my dear one,
    How shall we part?

He calls me, he cries
    Who is father to thee:
O birdeen, his eyes
    In these blue eyes I see.

Thou art wrought of our love,
    Of our joy that was slain:
My birdeen, my dove,
    My passion, my pain.

PULSE OF MY HEART

ARE these your eyes, Isla,
    That look into mine?
Is this smile, this laugh,
    Thine?

Heart of me, dear,
    O pulse of my heart,
This is our child, our child—
    And . . . we apart!

Wrought of thy life, Isla,
    Wrought in my womb,
Never to feel thy kiss!—
    Ah, bitter doom.

Hush, hush: within thine eyes
    His eyes I see. . . .
Soft as a bird's sighs
Thy breathings rise! . . .
    If there be Paradise
    For him and me
        (Who hold it but a dream
        Because of bitter fate)
The first supernal gleam
Beyond the flame-swept gate
Shall be thine eyes when thou drawest near—
None other shall it be
Who his lost hands, with mine, and thine
In love refound shall intertwine. . . .
But now, alas, alas, we are far apart,
    My baby dear,
        Pulse of my Heart!

The Rose of Flame

OH, fair immaculate rose of the world, rose of my dream, my Rose!
Beyond the ultimate gates of dream I have heard thy mystical call:
It is where the rainbow of hope suspends and the river of rapture
    flows—
And cool sweet dews from the wells of peace forever fall.

And all my heart is aflame because of the rapture and peace,
And I dream, in my waking dreams and deep in the dreams of sleep,
Till the high sweet wonderful call that shall be the call of release
Shall ring in my ears as I sink from gulf to gulf and from deep to
    deep—

Sink deep, sink deep beyond the ultimate dreams of all desire—
Beyond the uttermost limit of all that the craving spirit knows:
Then, then, oh then I shall be as the inner flame of thy fire,
O fair immaculate rose of the world, Rose of my Dream, my Rose!

The Undersong

    I HEAR the sea-song of the blood in my heart,
    I hear the sea-song of the blood in my ears:
    And I am far apart,
    And lost in the years.

    But when I lie and dream of that which was
    Before the first man's shadow flitted on the grass,
    I am stricken dumb
    With sense of that to come.

    Is then this wildering sea-song but a part
    Of the old song of the mystery of the years—
    Or only the echo of the tired heart
    And of tears?

The Lonely Hunter

GREEN branches, green branches, I see you beckon; I follow!
Sweet is the place you guard, there in the rowan-tree hollow.
There he lies in the darkness, under the frail white flowers,
Heedless at last, in the silence, of these sweet midsummer hours.

But sweeter, it may be, the moss whereon he is sleeping now,
And sweeter the fragrant flowers that may crown his moon-white brow:
And sweeter the shady place deep in an Eden hollow
Wherein he dreams I am with him—and dreaming, whispers, "Follow!"

Green wind from the green-gold branches, what is the song you bring?
What are all songs for me, now, who no more care to sing?
Deep in the heart of Summer, sweet is life to me still,
But my heart is a lonely hunter that hunts on a lonely hill.

Green is that hill and lonely, set far in a shadowy place;
White is the hunter's quarry, a lost-loved human face:
O hunting heart, shall you find it, with arrow of failing breath,
Led o'er a green hill lonely by the shadowy hound of Death?

Green branches, green branches, you sing of a sorrow olden,
But now it is midsummer weather, earth-young, sun-ripe, golden:
Here I stand and I wait, here in the rowan-tree hollow,
But never a green leaf whispers, "Follow, oh, Follow, Follow!"

O never a green leaf whispers, where the green-gold branches swing:
O never a song I hear now, where one was wont to sing.
Here in the heart of Summer, sweet is life to me still,
But my heart is a lonely hunter that hunts on a lonely hill.

THE WHITE PEACE

IT lies not on the sunlit hill
    Nor on the sunlit plain:
Nor ever on any running stream
    Nor on the unclouded main—

But sometimes, through the Soul of Man,
    Slow moving o'er his pain,
The moonlight of a perfect peace
    Floods heart and brain.

FROM THE HILLS OF DREAM

...... I would not find;
 For when I find, I know
I shall have claspt the wandering wind
 And built a house of snow."

FROM THE HILLS OF DREAM

ACROSS the silent stream
 Where the slumber-shadows go,
From the dim blue Hills of Dream
 I have heard the west wind blow.

Who hath seen that fragrant land,
 Who hath seen that unscanned west?
Only the listless hand
 And the unpulsing breast.

But when the west wind blows.
 I see moon-lances gleam
Where the Host of Faerie flows
 Athwart the Hills of Dream.

And a strange song I have heard
 By a shadowy stream,
And the singing of a snow-white bird
 On the Hills of Dream.

The Unknown Wind

("There is a wind that has no name."
Gaelic Saying.)

WHEN the day darkens,
    When dusk grows light,
When the dew is falling,
    When Silence dreams. . . .
I hear a wind
Calling, calling
By day and by night.

What is the wind
That I hear calling
By day and by night,
    The crying of wind?
When the day darkens,
When dusk grows light,
When the dew is falling?

Little Children of the Wind

I HEAR the little children of the wind
Crying solitary in lonely places:
I have not seen their faces
But I have seen the leaves eddying behind,
The little tremulous leaves of the wind.

A Milking Sian

GIVE up thy milk to her who calls
Across the low green hills of Heaven
And stream-cool meads of Paradise!

Across the low green hills of Heaven
How sweet to hear the milking call,
The milking call i' the meads of Heaven:

Stream-cool the meads of Paradise,
Across the low green hills of Heaven.

Give up thy milk to her who calls,
Sweet voiced amid the Starry Seven,
Give up thy milk to her who calls!

THE KYE-SONG OF ST. BRIDE

O SWEET St. Bride of the
    Yellow, yellow hair:
Paul said, and Peter said,
And all the saints alive or dead
Vowed she had the sweetest head,
Bonnie, sweet St. Bride of the
    Yellow, yellow hair.

White may my milking be,
    White as thee:
Thy face is white, thy neck is white,
Thy hands are white, thy feet are white,
For thy sweet soul is shining bright—
    O dear to me,
    O dear to see
    St. Bridget white!

Yellow may my butter be,
    Firm, and round:
Thy breasts are sweet,
Firm, round and sweet,
So may my butter be:
So may my butter be O
    Bridget sweet!

Safe thy way is, safe, O
    Safe, St. Bride:
May my kye come home at even,
None be fallin', none be leavin',
Dusky even, breath-sweet even,
Here, as there, where O
    St. Bride thou
Keepest tryst with God in heav'n,
Seest the angels bow
And souls be shriven—
Here, as there, 'tis breath-sweet even
    Far and wide—
Singeth thy little maid
Safe in thy shade
    Bridget, Bride!

ST. BRIDE'S LULLABY

OH, Baby Christ, so dear to me,
    Sang Bridget Bride:
How sweet thou art,
My baby dear,
Heart of my heart!

Heavy her body was with thee,
Mary, beloved of One in Three,
    Sang Bridget Bride—
Mary, who bore thee, little lad:
But light her heart was, light and glad
With God's love clad.

Sit on my knee,
    Sang Bridget Bride:
Sit here
O Baby dear,
Close to my heart, my heart:

For I thy foster-mother am,
My helpless lamb!
O have no fear,
    Sang good St. Bride.

None, none,
No fear have I:
So let me cling
Close to thy side
While thou dost sing,
O Bridget Bride!

My Lord, my Prince, I sing:
My Baby dear, my King!
    Sang Bridget Bride.

When the Dew is Falling

WHEN the dew is falling
I have heard a calling
Of aerial sweet voices o'er the low green hill;
And when the noon is dying
I have heard a crying
Where the brown burn slippeth thro' the hollows
    green and still.

And O the sorrow upon me,
The grey grief upon me,
For a voice that whispered once, and now for aye is
    still:
O heart forsaken, calling
When the dew is falling,
To the one that comes not ever o'er the low green hill.

INVOCATION OF PEACE

(After the Gaelic.)

DEEP peace I breathe into you,
O weariness, here:
O ache, here!
Deep peace, a soft white dove to you;
Deep peace, a quiet rain to you;
Deep peace, an ebbing wave to you!
Deep peace, red wind of the east from you;
Deep peace, grey wind of the west to you;
Deep peace, dark wind of the north from you;
Deep peace, blue wind of the south to you!
Deep peace, pure red of the flame to you;
Deep peace, pure white of the moon to you;
Deep peace, pure green of the grass to you;
Deep peace, pure brown of the earth to you;
Deep peace, pure grey of the dew to you,
Deep peace, pure blue of the sky to you!
Deep peace of the running wave to you,
Deep peace of the flowing air to you,
Deep peace of the quiet earth to you,
Deep peace of the sleeping stones to you!
Deep peace of the Yellow Shepherd to you,
Deep peace of the Wandering Shepherdess to you
Deep peace of the Flock of Stars to you,
Deep peace from the Son of Peace to you,
Deep pace from the heart of Mary to you,
From Bridget of the Mantle
Deep peace, deep peace!
And with the kindness too of the Haughty Father, Peace!
In the name of the Three who are One,
And by the will of the King of the Elements, Peace!
  Peace!

IN THE SILENCES OF THE WOODS

IN the silences of the woods
I have heard all day and all night
The moving multitudes
Of the Wind in flight.
He is named Myriad:
And I am sad
Often, and often I am glad,
But oftener I am white
With fear of the dim broods
That are his multitudes.

MATER CONSOLATRIX

HEART'S joy must fade . . . though it borrow
    Heaven's azure for its clay:
But the Joy that is one with Sorrow
    Treads an immortal way:
For each, is born To-Morrow,
    For each, is Yesterday.

Joy, that is clothed with shadow,
    Shall arise from the dead,
But Joy that is clothed with the rainbow
    Shall with the bow be sped: . . .
Where the Sun spends his fires is she,
    And where the Stars are led.

THE SOUL'S ARMAGEDDON

I KNOW not where I go,
O Wind, that calls afar:
O Wind that calls for war,
Where the Death-Moon doth glow
In a darkness without star.

Nor do I know the blare
Of the bugles that call:
Nor who rise, nor who fall:
Nor if the torches flare
Where the gods laugh, or crawl.

But I hear, I hear the hum,
The multitudinous cry,
Where myriads fly,
And I hear a voice say, Come:
And the same voice say, Die!

What is the war, O Wind?
Lo, without shield or spear
How can I draw near?
I am deaf and dumb and blind
With immeasurable fear.

Cantilena Mundi

WHERE rainbows rise through sunset rains
    By shores forlorn of isles forgot,
A solitary Voice complains
    'The World is here, the World is not.'

The Voice the wind is, or the sea,
    Or spirit of the sundown West:
Or is it but a breath set free
    From off the Islands of the Blest?

It may be: but I turn my face
    To that which still I hold so dear:
And lo, the voices of the days—
    'The World is not, the World is here.'

'Tis the same end whichever way,
    And either way is soon forgot:

'The World is all in all, To-day:
    To-morrow all the World is not.'

THE HILLS OF RUEL

"OVER the hills and far away"—
That is the tune I heard one day
When heather-drowsy I lay and listened
And watched where the stealthy sea-tide glistened

Beside me there on the Hills of Ruel
An old man stooped and gathered fuel—
And I asked him this: if his son were dead,
As the folk in Glendaruel all said,
How could he still believe that never
Duncan had crossed the shadowy river.

Forth from his breast the old man drew
A lute that once on a rowan-tree grew;
And, speaking no words, began to play
"Over the hills and far away."

"But how do you know," I said thereafter,
"That Duncan has heard the fairy laughter?
How do you know he has followed the cruel
Honey-sweet folk of the Hills of Ruel?"
"How do I know?" the old man said,
"Sure I know well my boy 's not dead:
For late on the morrow they hid him, there
Where the black earth moistens his yellow hair,
I saw him alow on the moor close by,
I watched him low on the hillside lie,
An' I heard him laughin' wild up there,
An' talk, talk, talkin' beneath his hair—

For down o'er his face his long hair lay
But I saw it was cold and ashy grey.

Ay, laughin' and talkin' wild he was,
An' that to a Shadow out on the grass,
A Shadow that made my blood go chill,
For never its like have I seen on the hill.
An' the moon came up, and the stars grew white,
An' the hills grew black in the bloom o' the night,
An' I watched till the death-star sank in the moon
And the moonmaid fled with her flittermice shoon,
Then the Shadow that lay on the moorside there
Rose up and shook its wildmoss hair,
And Duncan he laughed no more, but grey
As the rainy dust of a rainy day,
Went over the hills and far away."

"Over the hills and far away"
That is the tune I heard one day.
O that I too might hear the cruel
Honey-sweet folk of the Hills of Ruel.

THE BUGLES OF DREAMLAND

SWIFTLY the dews of the gloaming are falling:
Faintly the bugles of Dreamland are calling.
   O hearken, my darling, the elf-flutes are blowing
   The shining-eyed folk from the hillside are flowing,
   I' the moonshine the wild-apple blossoms are snowing,
   And louder and louder where the white dews are falling
   The far-away bugles of Dreamland are calling.

O what are the bugles of Dreamland calling
There where the dews of the gloaming are falling?
   Come away from the weary old world of tears,
   Come away, come away to where one never hears
   The slow weary drip of the slow weary years,
   But peace and deep rest till the white dews are falling
   And the blithe bugle-laughters through Dreamland are calling.

Then bugle for us, where the cool dews are falling,
O bugle for us, wild elf-flutes now calling—
    For Heart's-love and I are too weary to wait
    For the dim drowsy whisper that cometh too late,
    The dim muffled whisper of blind empty fate—
    O the world's well lost now the dream-dews are falling,
    And the bugles of Dreamland about us are calling.

DALUA[3]

I HAVE heard you calling, Dalua,
              Dalua!
I have heard you on the hill,
By the pool-side still,
Where the lapwings shrill
    Dalua ... dalua ... dalua!

What is it you call, Dalua,
              Dalua?
When the rains fall,
When the mists crawl
And the curlews call
    Dalua ... dalua ... dalua!

I am the Fool, Dalua,
              Dalua!
When men hear me, their eyes
Darken: the shadow in the skies
Droops: and the keening-woman cries
    DALUA ... DALUA ... DALUA!

---

[3] Dalua, one of the names of a mysterious being in the Celtic mythology, the Fairy Fool.

The Lords of Shadow

WHERE the water whispers mid the shadowy rowan-trees
I have heard the Hidden People like the hum of swarming bees:
And when the moon has risen and the brown burn glisters grey
I have seen the Green Host marching in laughing disarray.

Dalua then must sure have blown a sudden magic air
Or with the mystic dew have sealed my eyes from seeing fair:
For the great Lords of Shadow who tread the deeps of night
Are no frail puny folk who move in dread of mortal sight.

For sure Dalua laughed alow, Dalua the fairy Fool,
When with his wildfire eyes he saw me 'neath the rowan-shadowed
    pool:
His touch can make the chords of life a bitter jangling tune,
The false glows true, the true glows false, beneath his moontide rune.

The laughter of the Hidden Host is terrible to hear,
The Hounds of Death would harry me at lifting of a spear:
Mayhap Dalua made for me the hum of swarming bees
And sealed my eyes with dew beneath the shadowy rowan-trees.

Morag of the Glen

    WHEN Morag of the Glen was fëy
    They took her where the Green Folk stray:
    And there they left her, night and day,
    A day and night they left her, fëy.

    And when they brought her home again,
    Aye of the Green Folk was she fain:
    They brought her leannan, Roy M'Lean,
    She looked at him with proud disdain.

    For I have killed a man, she said,
    A better man than you to wed:

I slew him when he clasped my head,
And now he sleepeth with the dead.

And did you see that little wren?
My sister dear it was flew, then!
That skull her home, that eye her den,
Her song is, *Morag o' the Glen!*

For when she went I did not go,
But washed my hands in blood-red woe:
O wren, trill out your sweet song's flow,
Morag is white as the driven snow!

THE MOON-CHILD

A LITTLE lonely child am I
    That have not any soul:
God made me as the homeless wave,
    That has no goal.

A seal my father was, a seal
    That once was man:
My mother loved him tho' he was
    'Neath mortal ban.

He took a wave and drowned her,
    She took a wave and lifted him:
And I was born where shadows are
    In sea-depths dim.

All through the sunny blue-sweet hours
    I swim and glide in waters green:
Never by day the mournful shores
    By me are seen.

But when the gloom is on the wave
    A shell unto the shore I bring:

And then upon the rocks I sit
    And plaintive sing.

I have no playmate but the tide
      The seaweed loves with dark brown eyes:
The night-waves have the stars for play,
    For me but sighs.

The Rune of the Four Winds

BY the Voice in the corries
When the Polestar danceth:

By the Voice on the summits
The dead feet know:

By the soft wet cry
When the Heat-star troubleth:

By the plaining and moaning
Of the Sigh of the Rainbows:

By the four white winds of the world,
Whose father the golden Sun is,
Whose mother the wheeling Moon is,
The North and the South and the East and the West
By the four good winds of the world,
That Man knoweth,
That One dreadeth,
That God blesseth—

        Be all well
           On mountain and moorland and lea
        On loch-face and lochan and river,
          On shore and shallow and sea!

By the Voice of the Hollow
Where the worm dwelleth:

By the Voice of the Hollow
Where the sea-wave stirs not:

By the Voice of the Hollow
That sun hath not seen yet:

By the three dark winds of the world;
The chill dull breath of the Grave,
The breath from the depths of the Sea,
The breath of To-morrow:
By the white and dark winds of the world,
The four and the three that are seven,
That Man knoweth,
That One dreadeth,
That God blesseth—

    Be all well
      On mountain and moorland and lea,
     On loch-face and lochan and river,
       On shore and shallow and sea!

Naoi Miannain

MIANN mna sithe, braon:
Miann Sluagh, gaoth:
Miann fitheach, fuil:
Miann eunarag, an fasaich:
Miann faoileag, faileagan mhara:
Miann Bàrd, fith-cheol-min lhuchd nan trusganan uaine:
Miann fear, gaol bhean:
Miann mna, chlann beag:
Miann arrama, ais.

NINE DESIRES

THE desire of the fairy women, dew:
The desire of the fairy host, wind:
The desire of the raven, blood:
The desire of the snipe, the wilderness:
The desire of the seamew, the lawns of the sea:
The desire of the poet, the soft low music of the
    Tribe of The Green Mantles:
The desire of man, the love of woman:
The desire of women, the little clan:
The desire of the soul, wisdom.

FOAM OF THE PAST

THRENODIES AND SONGS
CHANTS AND DIRGES

To W. B. Yeats

IN a small book in a greater, "The Little Book of the Great Enchantment" in *The Book of White Magic (or Wisdom)* . . . the "Leabhran Mhòr Gheasadaireachd" to give the Gaelic name . . . it is said: "When have you a memory out of darkness, tell to a seer, to a poet, and to a friend, that which you remember: and if the seer say, I see it—and if the poet say, I hear it—and if the friend say, I believe it: then know of a surety that your remembrance is a true remembrance." But if our ancestral memories, or memories of the imagination, or reveries of the imagining mind wandering in a world publicly foregone yet inwardly actual, could become authentic only by a test such as this, then I fear they would indeed be apparent as mere foam, the froth dream. For where is he who is at once seer and poet and friend? Well, you have the great desire, which is the threshold of vision, and vision itself you have, which is the white enchantment: your words that you compel to a new and subtle music, and the unknown airs in your mind that shepherd those words into the green glens of your imagination, would reveal you as the poet, though not one of your fellows acclaimed you, or none offered you the mistletoe bough with its old symbolism of wisdom and song: and, finally, I think I may call you friend, for we go one way, the dearer that it is narrow and little trod and leads by the whispering sedge and the wilderness, and meet sometimes on that way, and know that we seek the same Graal, and shall come upon it, beyond that fathomless hollow of green water that lies in the West as our poets say, the "Pool" whose breath is Silence and over which hangs a bow of red flame whitening to its moonwhite core.

So you, perhaps, may say of some of these lines in "From the Hills of Dream" and "Foam of the Past" that they come familiarly to you in other than the sense of mere acquaintance. I think you too have known the dew which falls when Dalua whispers under the shadowy rowan-trees, and have heard the laughter of the Hidden Host. and known, ... not the fairie folk of later legend, ... but the perilous passage of the great Lords of Shadow who 'tread the deeps of night.' You, too, perhaps, have feared The White Hound and the Red Shepherd: and have known that weariness, too old and deep for words, of which the aged Gaelic woman of the Island of Tiree had dim knowledge when she sang

> *It is the grey rock I am,*
> *And the grey rain on the rock:*
> *It is the grey wave ...*
> *That grey bound.*

You have heard The Rune of the Winds, the blowing of the four white winds and the three dark winds: perhaps, if you have not seen, or heard, my little Moon-Child, you remember her from long ago, and her loneliness when she sang

> *I have no playmate but the tide*
> *The seaweed tones with dark brown eyes:*
> *The night-waves have the stars for play,*
> *For me but sighs.*

For all poetry is in a sense memory: all art, indeed, is a mnemonic gathering of the innumerable and lost into the found and unique. I am sure that you, too, have seen the rising of the Crimson Moon, and have walked secretly with Midir of the Dew and moon-crown'd Brigid and wave-footed Mànan. For you also the long way that seems brief and the short way that seems long, who can say with Dalua (in *The Immortal Hour*)

> *And if I tread the long, continuous way*
> *Within a narrow round, not thinking it long,*
> *And fare a single hour thinking it many days,*
> *I am not first or last of the Immortal Clan,*
> *For whom the long ways of the world are brief*
> *And the short ways hem with unimagined time.*

So that to you, for one, these poems, however rude in form they may sometimes be, will come with that remembrance of the imagination which is the incalculable air of the otherworld of poetry. As you know, most of them have their place in tales of mine coloured with the colour of a lost day and of a beauty that is legend: and must suffer by severance from their context, as pluckt pine-branches lose, if not their native savour, at least the light and gloom of their forest-company and the smooth hand of the wind. The sound and colour of a barbarous day may well vanish in these broken recalling strains . . . at their best dimly caught even when, for example, 'The Death Dance' be read in its due place in "The Laughter of the Queen," apart from which it is perhaps like an air born a thousand years ago on a Gaelic minstrel's clarsach and played anew to-day with curious artifice on a many-noted instrument. One or two at least of these threnodies and chants will have for you the familiar cadence of thought as well as of the fall of words, for they are but adaptations of what long ago were chanted to rude harps made of applewood and yew. The songs of the Swan-Children of Lir have been sung by many poets: Deirdre's Lament on leaving Scotland, as she and Nathos (Naois) crossed the Irish Sea, has been a music in every generation of the Gael: and I do no more than remember, and repeat, with an accent of atmosphere or thought or words, which, perhaps, just reveals the difference between paraphrase and metaphrase. Like Deirdre, we, too, look often yearningly to a land from which we are exiled in time, but inhabit in dream and longing, saying with her

> *Glen of the Roes, Glen of the Roes,*
> *In thee I have dreamed to the full my happy dream:*
> *O that where the shallow bickering Ruel flows*
> *I might hear again, o'er its flashing gleam,*
> *The cuckoos calling by the murmuring stream.*

F. M.

WHITE-HANDS

O WHERE in the north, or where in the south, or where in the east or west
Is she who hath the flower-white hands and the swandown breast?
O, if she be west, or east she be, or in the north or south,
A sword will leap, a horse will prance, ere I win to Honey-Mouth.

She has great eyes, like the doe on the hill, and warm and sweet she is,
O, come to me, Honey-Mouth, bend to me, Honey-Mouth, give me thy kiss!

White Hands her name is, where she reigns amid the princes fair:
White hands she moves like swimming swans athrough her dusk-wave hair:
White hands she puts about my heart, white hands fan up my breath:
White hands take out the heart of me, and grant me life or death!

White hands make better songs than hymns, white hands are young and sweet:
O, a sword for me, O Honey-Mouth, and a war-horse fleet!
O wild sweet eyes! O glad wild eyes! O mouth, how sweet it is!
O, come to me, Honey-Mouth! bend to me, Honey-Mouth! give me thy kiss!

HEART O' BEAUTY

O WHERE are thy white hands, Heart o' Beauty?
                                Heart o' Beauty!
They are as white foam on the swept sands,
                                Heart o' Beauty!
They are as white swans i' the dusk, thy white hands,
Wild swans in flight over shadowy lands,
                                Heart o' Beauty!

O lift again thy white hands, Heart o' Beauty,
                                Heart o' Beauty!

Harp to the white waves on the yellow sands,
> Heart o' Beauty!

They will hearken now to these waving wands,
To the magic wands of thy white hands,
> Heart o' Beauty!

From the white dawn till the grey dusk,
> Heart o' Beauty!

I hear the unseen waves of unseen strands,
> Heart o' Beauty!

I see the sun rise and set over shadowy lands,
But never, never, never thy white hands, thy white hands,
> Heart o' Beauty!

OONA OF THE DARK EYES AND THE CRYING OF WIND

I HAVE fared far in the dim woods:
And I have known sorrow and grief,
And the incalculable years
That haunt the solitudes.
Where now are the multitudes
Of the Field of Spears?
Old tears
Fall upon them as rain,
Their eyes are quiet under the brown leaf.

I have seen the dead, innumerous:
I too shall lie thus,
And thou, Congal, thou too shalt lie
Still and white
Under the starry sky,
And rise no more to any Field of Spears,
But, under the brown leaf,
Remember grief
And the old, salt, bitter tears.

And I have heard the crying of wind
It is the crying that is in my heart:
Oona of the Dark Eyes, Oona of the Dark
Oona, Oona, Oona, Heart of my Heart!
But there is only crying of wind
Through the silences of the sky,
Dews that fall and rise,
The faring of long years,
And the coverlet of the brown leaf
For the old familiar grief
And the old tears.

The Lament of Ian the Proud

WHAT is this crying that I hear in the wind?
Is it the old sorrow and the old grief?
Or is it a new thing coming, a whirling leaf
About the grey hair of me who am weary and blind?
I know not what it is, but on the moor above the shore
There is a stone which the purple nets of the heather bind,
And thereon is writ: *She will return no mere.*
O blown whirling leaf,
And the old grief,
And wind crying to me who am old and blind!

The Monody of Isla the Singer

"Like Bells on the wind..."

Is it time to let the Hour rise and go forth as a hound loosed from the battle-cars?
Is it time to let the Hour go forth, as the White Hound with the eyes of flame?
For if it be not time I would have this hour that is left to me under the stars
Wherein I may dream my dream again, and at the last whisper one name.

It is the name of one who was more fair than youth to the old, than life
    to the young:
She was more fair than the first love of Angus the Beautiful, and though
    I were blind
And deaf for a hundred ages I would see her, more fair than any poet
    has sung,
And hear her voice like mournful bells crying on the wind.

The End of Aodh-of-the-Songs

THE swift years slip and slide adown the steep;
The slow years pass; neither will come again.
You huddled years have weary eyes that weep,
These laugh, these moan, these silent frown, these plain,
These have their lips curl'd up with proud disdain.

O years with tears, and tears through weary years,
How weary I who in your arms have lain:
Now, I am tired: the sound of slipping spears
Moves soft, and tears fall in a bloody rain,
And the chill footless years go over me who am slain.

I hear, as in a wood, dim with old light, the rain,
Slow falling; old, old, weary, human tears:
And in the deepening dark my comfort is my Pain,
Sole comfort left of all my hopes and fears,
Pain that alone survives, gaunt hound of the shadowy years.

The Love-chant of Cormac Conlingas

OIMÉ, Oimé woman of the white breasts, Eilidh![4]
Woman of the golden hair, and lips of the red, red rowan!
        Oimé, O-rì, Oimé!

Where is the swan that is whiter, with breast more smooth,
Or the wave on the sea that moves as thou movest, Eilidh—
        Oimé, a-rò; Oimé, a-rò!

It is the marrow in my bones that is aching, aching, Eilidh:
It is the blood in my body that is a bitter wild tide, Oimé!
        O-rì, Ohion, O-rì, aròne!

Is it the heart of thee calling that I am hearing, Eilidh,
Or the wind in the wood, or the beating of the sea, Eilidh,
        Or the beating of the sea?

Shule, shule agràh, shule agràh, shule agràh, Shule!
Heart of me, move to me! move to me, heart of me, Eilidh, Eilidh,
        Move to me!

Ah! let the wild hawk take it, the name of me, Cormac Conlingas,
Take it and tear at thy heart with it, heart that of old was so hot with
   it,
        Eilidh, Eilidh, O-rì, Eilidh, Eilidh!

The Washer of the Ford

THERE is a lonely stream afar in a lone dim land:
It hath white dust for shore it has, white bones bestrew the strand:
The only thing that liveth there is a naked leaping sword;
But I, who a seer am, have seen the whirling hand
        Of the Washer of the Ford.

---

[4] Eilidh is pronounced Eily.

A shadowy shape of cloud and mist, of gloom and dusk, she stands,
                The Washer of the Ford:
She laughs, at times, and strews the dust through the hollow of her hands.
She counts the sins of all men there, and slays the red-stained horde—
The ghosts of all the sins of men must know the whirling sword
                Of the Washer of the Ford.

She stoops and laughs when in the dust she sees a writhing limb:
"Go back into the ford," she says, "and hither and thither swim;
Then I shall wash you white as snow, and shall take you by the hand,
And slay you here in the silence with this my whirling brand,
And trample you into the dust of this white windless sand"—
                This is the laughing word
                Of the Washer of the Ford
                Along that silent strand.

THE DEATH-DIRGE FOR CATHAL

OUT of the wild hills I am hearing a voice, O Cathal!
And I am thinking it is the voice of a bleeding sword.
Whose is that sword? I know it well: it is the sword of the Slayer—
Him that is called Death, and the song that it sings I know:—
O where is Cathal mac Art, the white cup for the thirst of my lips?

Out of the cold greyness of the sea I am hearing, O Cathal,
I am hearing a wave-muffled voice, as of one who drowns in the depths:
Whose is that voice? I know it well: it is the voice of the Shadow—
Her that is called the Grave, and the song that she sings I know:—
O where is Cathal mac Art, that has warmth for the chill that I have?

Out of the hot greenness of the wood I am hearing, O Cathal,
I am hearing a rustling step, as of one stumbling blind.
Whose is that rustling step? I know it well: the rustling walk of the Blind
    One—
She that is called Silence, and the song that she sings I know:—
O where is Cathal mac Art, that has tears water my stillness?

The Moon-Song of Cathal

O YELLOW lamp of Iona that is having a cold pale flame there,
Put thy honey-sheen upon me who am close-caverned with Death:
Sure it is little I see now who have seen too much and too little:
O moon, thy breast is softer and whiter than hers who burneth the day.

Put thy white light on the grave where the dead man my father is,
And waken him, waken him, wake!
And put thy soft shining on the breast of the woman my mother,
So that she stir in her sleep and say to the viking beside her,
"Take up thy sword, and let it lap blood, for it thirsts with long thirst."

And O Ioua, be as the sea-calm upon the hot heart of Ardanna, the girl:
Tell her that Cathal loves her, and that memory is sweeter than life.
I hear her heart beating here in the dark and the silence,
And it is not lonely I am, because of that, and remembrance.

O yellow flame of Ioua, be a spilling of blood out of the heart of Ecta,
So that he fall dead, inglorious, slain from within, as a greybeard;
And light a fire in the brain of Molios, so that he shall go moonstruck,
And men will jeer at him, and he will die at the last, idly laughing!

For lo, I worship thee, Ioua; and if thou canst give my message to Neis,—
Neis the helot out of Iondu, Neis of Iona, bondman to Colum,—
Tell him I hail thee as Bandia, as god-queen and mighty,
And that he had the wisdom and I was a fool with trickling ears of moss.

But grant me this, O goddess, a bitter moon-drinking for Colum!
May he have the moonsong in his brain, and in his heart the moonfire:
Flame take him to heart of flame, and may he wane as wax at the furnace,
And his soul drown in tears, and his body be a nothingness upon the
    sands!

The Sun-Chant Of Cathal

O HOT yellow fire that streams out of the sky, sword-white and golden,
Be a flame upon the monks that are praying in their cells in Iona!
Be a fire in the veins of Colum, and the hell that he preacheth be his,
And be a torch to the men of Lochlin that they discover the isle and
    consume it!

For I see this thing, that the old gods are the gods that die not:
All else is a seeming, a dream, a madness, a tide ever ebbing.
Glory to thee, O Grian, lord of life, first of the gods, Allfather,
Swords and spears are thy beams, thy breath a fire that consumeth!

And upon this isle of A-rinn send sorrow and death and disaster,
Upon one and all save Ardanna, who gave me her bosom,
Upon one and all send death, the curse of a death slow and swordless,
From Molios of the Cave to Mûrta and Diarmid my doomsmen!

The Song of Fionula

(From "*The Swan-Children of Lir.*")

HAPPY our father Lir afar,
With mead, and songs of love and war:
The salt brine, and the white foam,
With these his children have their home.

In the sweet days of long ago
Soft-clad we wandered to and fro:
But now cold winds of dawn and night
Pierce deep our feathers thin and light.

The hazel mead in cups of gold
We feasted from in days of old:
The sea-weed now our food, our wine
The salt, keen, bitter, barren brine.

On soft warm couches once we pressed:
White harpers lulled us to our rest:
Our beds are now where the sea raves,
Our lullaby the clash of waves.

Alas! the fair sweet days are gone
When love was ours from dawn to dawn:
Our sole companion now is pain,
Through frost and snow, through storm and rain.

Beneath my wings my brothers lie
When the fierce ice-winds hurtle by:
On either side and 'neath my breast
Lir's sons have known no other rest.

Ah, kisses we shall no more know,
Ah, love so dear exchanged for woe,
All that is sweet for us is o'er,
Homeless we are from shore to shore.

THE CHANT OF ARDAN THE PICT

O COLUM and monks of Christ,
It is peace we are having this night:
Sure, peace is a good thing,
And I am glad with the gladness.

We worship one God,
Though ye call him Dia—
And I say not, o Dhê!
But cry Bea'uil!

For it is one faith for man,
And one for the living world,
And no man is wiser than another—
And none knoweth much.

None knoweth a better thing than this:
The Sword, Love, Song, Honour, Sleep.
None knoweth a surer thing than this:
Birth, Sorrow, Pain, Weariness, Death.

Sure, peace is a good thing;
Let us be glad of peace:
We are not men of the Sword,
But of the Rune and the Wisdom.

I have learned a truth of Colum,
He hath learned of me:
All ye on the morrow shall see
A wonder of the wonders.

The thought is on you, that the Cross
Is known only of you:
Lo, I tell you the birds know it
That are marked with the Sorrow.

Listen to the Birds of Sorrow,
They shall tell you a great Joy:
It is Peace you will be having,
With the Birds.

The Song of Deirdrê

Ionmhuin tir, an tir ud shoir—
Alba go na h'-iongantaibh;
Nocha ttiocfainn aiste ale,
Muna ttagainn le Naoise.

O WOODS of Oona, I can hear the singing
Of the west wind among the branches green
And the leaping and laughing of cool waters springing,
And my heart aches for all that has been,
For all that has been, my Home, all that has been!

Glenmassan! O Glenmassan!
High the sorrel there, and the sweet fragrant grasses:
It would be well if I were listening now to where
In Glenmassan the sun shines and the cool we passes,
Glenmassan of the grasses!

Loch Etive, O fair Loch Etive, that was my first home,
I think of thee now when on the grey-green sea—
And beneath the mist in my eyes and the flying
I look back wearily,
I look back wearily to thee!

Glen Orchy, O Glen Orchy, fair sweet glen,
Was ever I more happy than in thy shade?
Was not Nathos there the happiest of men?
O may thy beauty never fade,
Most fair and sweet and beautiful glade.

Glen of the Roes, Glen of the Roes,
In thee I have dreamed to the full my happy dream:
O that where the shallow bickering Ruel flows,
I might hear again, o'er its flashing gleam,
The cuckoos calling by the murmuring stream.

THE DEATH SHADOW

OH, death of Fergus, that is lying in the boat here,
    Betwixt the man of the red hair and him of the black beard,
Rise now, and out of thy cold white eyes take out the fear,
    And let Fergus mac Art mhic Fheargus see his weird!

Sure, now, it's a blind man I am, but I'm thinking I see
    The shadow of you crawling across the dead.
Soon you will twine your arm around his shaking knee,
    And be whispering your silence into his listless head.

The Meditation of Colum

Before the Miracle of the Fishes and the Flies.

PRAISE be to God, and a blessing too at that, and a blessing!
For Colum the White, Colum the Dove, hath worshipped;
Yea he hath worshipped and made of a desert a garden,
And out of the dung of men's souls hath made a sweet
    savour of burning.

II

A savour of burning, most sweet, a fire for the altar,
This he hath made in the desert; the hell-saved all gladden.
Sure he hath put his benison, too, on milch-cow and
    bullock,
On the fowls of the air, and the man-eyed seals, and the
    otter.

III

But where in his Dûn in the great blue mainland of Heaven
God the Allfather broodeth, where the harpers are harping
    His glory;
There where He sitteth, where a river of ale poureth ever,
His great sword broken, His spear in the dust, He broodeth.

IV

And this is the thought that moves in His brain, as a cloud
    filled with thunder
Moves through the vast hollow sky filled with the dust of
    the stars
What boots it the glory of Colum, since he maketh a
    Sabbath to bless me
And hath no thought of my sons in the deeps of the air and
    the sea?

The Lamentation of Balva the Monk

BALVA the old monk I am called: when I was young, Balva Honeymouth.
That was before Colum the White came to Iona in the West.
She whom I loved was a woman whom I won out of the South,
And I had a good heaven with my lips on hers and with breast to breast.

Balva the old monk I am called: were it not for the fear
That the Soul of Colum the White would meet my soul in the Narrows
That sever the living and dead, I would rise up from here
And go back to where men pray with spears and arrows.

Balva the old monk I am called: ugh! ugh! the cold bell of the matins—'tis dawn!
Sure it's a dream I have had that I was in a warm wood with the sun ashine,
And that against me in the pleasant greenness was a soft fawn,
And a voice that whispered 'Balva Honey-mouth, drink, I am thy wine!'

The Last Night of Artân the Culdee

IT is but a little thing to sit here in the silence and the dark:
For I remember the blazing noon when I saw Oona the White:
I remember the day when we sailed the Moyle in our skin-built barque;
And I remember when Oona's lips were on mine in the heart of the night.

So it is a little thing to sit here, hearing nought, seeing nought:
When the dawn breaks they will hurry me hence to the new-dug grave:
It will be quiet there, if it be true what the good Colum has taught,
And I shall hear Oona's voice as a sleeping seal hears the moving wave.

The Death Dance

O ARONE a-ree, eily arone, arone!
'Tis a good thing to be sailing across the seas!
How the women smile and the children are laughing glad
When the galleys go out into the blue sea—atone!
        O eily arone, atone!

But the children may laugh less when the wolves come,
And the women may smile less in the winter-cold—
For the Summer-sailors will not come again, arone!
        O arone a-ree, eily arone, arone!

I am thinking they will not sail back again, O no!
The yellow-haired men that came sailing across the sea:
For 'tis wild apples they would be, and swing on green branches,
And sway in the wind for the corbies to preen their eyne,
        O eily arone, eily a-ree!

And it is pleasure for Scathach the Queen to see this:
To see the good fruit that grows on the Tree of the Stones:
Long black fruit it is, wind-swayed by its yellow roots,
And like men they are with their feet dancing in the void air!
        O, O, arone, a-ree, eily arone!

O arone a-ree, eily arone, arone,
O, O, arone, a-ree, eily arone!

The Song of Ahez the Pale

BUT this was in the old, old, far-off, days,
But this was in the old, old, far-off days.

They rode beneath the ancient boughs, and as they rode she sang,
But at the last both silent were: only the horse-hoofs rang.

Guenn took up his sword, and she felt its shining blade,
And she laughed and vowed it fitted ill for the handling of a maid.

He looked at her, and darkly smiled, and said she was a queen:
For she could swing the white sword high and love its dazzling sheen.

She lifted up the great white sword and swung it o'er his head—
"Ah, you may smile, my lord, now you may smile," she said.

For this was in the old, old, far-off days,
For this was in the old, old, far-off days.

CLOSING DOORS

CLOSING DOORS

O SANDS of my heart, what wind moans low along thy shadowy
    shore?
Is that the deep sea-heart I hear with the dying sob at its core?
Each dim lost wave that lapses is like a closing door:
'Tis closing doors they hear at last who soon shall hear no more,
              Who soon shall hear no more.

Eily, Eily, Eily, call low, come back, call low to me:
My heart you have broken, your troth for-saken, but love even yet can
    be:
Come near, call low, for closing doors are as the waves o' the sea,
Once closed they are closed for ever, Eily, lost, lost, for thee and me,
              Lost, lost, for thee and me.

THE STAR OF BEAUTY

    IT dwells not in the skies,
          My Star of Beauty!
    'Twas made of her sighs,
    Her tears and agonies,
    The fire in her eyes,
          My Star of Beauty!

Lovely and delicate,
          My Star of Beauty!
How could she master Fate,
Although she gave back hate
Great as my love was great,
          My Star of Beauty!

> I loved, she hated, well:
> > My Star of Beauty!
> Soon, soon the passing bell:
> She rose, and I fell:
> Soft shines in deeps of hell
> > My Star of Beauty!

In the Shadow

O SHE will have the deep dark heart, for all her face is fair;
As deep and dark as though beneath the shadow of her hair:
For in her hair a spirit dwells that no white spirit is,
And hell is in the hopeless heaven of that lost spirit's kiss.

She has two men within the palm, the hollow of her hand:
She takes their souls and blows them forth as idle drifted sand:
And one falls back upon her breast that is his quiet home,
And one goes out into the night and is as wind-blown foam.

And when she sees the sleep of one, oft-times she rises there
And looks into the outer dark and calleth soft and fair:
And then the lost soul that afar within the dark doth roam
Comes laughing, laughing, laughing, and crying, Home! Home!

There is no home in faithless love, O fool that dreams her fair:
Bitter and drear that home you seek, the name of it Despair:
Drown, drown beneath the sterile kiss of the engulfing wave,
A heaven of peace it is beside this mockery of a grave.

The Cup

Chuir Muiril mirr ann,
Chuir Uiril mil ann,
Chuir Muirinn fion ann,
'Schuir Michal ann huadh.

"Muriel placed myrrh in it:
Uriel placed honey in it:
Murien placed wine in it:
And Michael power."

THE cup of bitter-sweet I know
That with old wine of love doth glow:
The dew of tears to it doth go,
And wisdom is its hidden woe.

Were I but young again to throw
This cup where the wild thistles grow,
Or where, oblivious, ceaseless, slow,
The grey tumultuous waters flow!

An Old Tale of Three

AH, bonnie darling, lift your dark eyes dreaming!
See, the firelight fills the gloaming, though deep darkness
    grows without—

[Hush, dear, hush, I hear the sea-birds screaming,
And down beyond the haven the tide comes with a shout!]

Ah, birdeen, sweetheart, sure he is not coming,
He who has your hand in his, while I have all your heart—

[Hush, dear, hush, I hear the wild bees humming
Far away in the underworld where true love shall not part!]

Darling, darling, darling, all the world is singing,
Singing, singing, singing a song of joy for me!

[Hush, dear, hush, what wild sea-wind is bringing
Gloom o' the sea about thy brow, athwart the eyes of thee?]

Ah, heart o' me, darling, darling, all my heart's aflame!
Sure, at the last we are all in all, all in all we two!

At the Door

A VOICE

This is the way I take my own, this is the boon I claim!
Sure at the last, ye are all in all, all in all, ye two—

(Later, in the dark, the living brooding beside the dead:—)

Ah, hell of my heart! Ye are dust to me—and dust with dust may woo!

THE CRIMSON MOON

BEHIND the Legions of the Sun, the Star Battalions of the night,
The reddening of the West I see, from morn till dusk, from dusk till light.
A day must surely come at last, and that day soon,
When the Hidden People shall march out beneath the Crimson Moon.

Our palaces shall crumble then, our towers shall fall away,
And on the plains our burning towns shall flaunt a desolate day:
The cities of our pride shall wear tiaras of red flame,
And all our phantom glory be an idle windblown name.

What shall our vaunt be on that day, or who thereon shall hear
The laughter of our laughing lips become the wail of fear?

Our vaunt shall be the windy dust in eddies far and wide,
The hearing, theirs who follow us with swift and dreadful stride.

A cry of lamentation, then, shall sweep from land to land:
A myriad wavering hands shall shake above a myriad strand:
The Day shall swoon before a Shade of vast ancestral Night,
Till a more dreadful Morn awake to flood and spume of light.

This is the prophecy of old, before the running tribes of Man
Spread Multitude athwart the heirdom of an earlier Clan—
Before the gods drank Silence, and hid their way with cloud,
And Man uprose and claimed the Earth and all the starry crowd.

So Man conceived and made his dream, till at the last he smiled to see
Its radiant skirts brush back the stars from Immortality:
He crowned himself with the Infinite, and gave his Soul a Home,
And then the quiet gods awoke and blew his life to foam.

This is the Dream I see anew, when all the West is red with light,
Behind the Legions of the Sun, the Star Battalions of the night.
Verily the day may come at last, and that day soon,
When the Hidden People shall march out beneath the Crimson
    Moon.

The Tryst of Queen Hynde

QUEEN Hynde was in the rowan-wood with scarlet fruit aflame,
Her face was as the berries were, one sun-hot wave of shame.

With scythes of fire the August sun mowed down vast swathes of
    shade:
With blazing eyes the waiting queen stared on her steel-blue blade.

"What thirsty hound," she muttered low, "with thirst you flash and
    gleam:
Bide, bide a wee, my bonnie hound, I'll show ye soon a stream!"

The sun had tossed against the West his broken scythes of fire
When Lord Gillanders bowed before his Queen and Sweet Desire.

She did not give him smile or kiss; her hand she did not give:
"But are ye come for death," she said, "or are ye come to live?"

Gillanders reined and looked at her: "Hynde, Queen and Love," he said,
"I wooed in love, I come in love, to this the tryst we made:

"Why are your eyes so fierce and wild: why is your face so white:
I love you with all my love," he said, "by day and by night."

"What o' the word that's come to me, of how my lord's to wed
The lilywhite maid o' one that has a gold crown on his head?

"What o' the word that yesternight ye wan-toned with my name,
And on a windy scorn let loose the blown leaf o' my shame?"

The Lord Gillanders looked at her, and never a word said be,
But sprang from off his great black horse and sank upon his knee.

"This is my love," said white Queen Hynde, "and this, and this, and this"—
Four times she stabbed him to the heart while she his lips did kiss.

She left him in the darkling wood: and as she rode she sang
(The little notes swirled in and out amid the horse-hoof clang)

My love was sweet, was sweet, was meet, but not so sweet as now!
A deep long sleep my sweet love has beneath the rowan-bough.

They let her in, they lifted swords, his head each one did bare:
Slowly she bowed, slowly she passed, slowly she clomb the stair:

Her little son she lifted up, and whispered 'neath his cries—
'The old king's son, they say; mayhap he has Gillander's eyes."

THE LOVE-KISS OF DERMID AND GRAINNE

WHEN by the twilit sea these twain were come
Dermid spake no one word, Grainne was dumb
And in the hearts of both deep silence was.
"Sorrow upon me, love," whispered the grass;
"Sorrow upon me, love," the sea-bird cried;
"Sorrow upon me, love," the lapsed wave sighed.

"For what the King has willed, that thing must be,
O Dermid! As two waves upon this sea
Wind-swept we are,—the wind of his dark mind,
With fierce inevitable tides behind."
"What would you have, O Grainne: he is King."
"I would we were the birds that come with Spring,
The purple-feathered birds that have no home,
The birds that love, then fly across the foam."

"Give me thy mouth, O Dermid," Grainne said
Thereafter, and whispering thus she leaned her head—
Ah, supple, subtle snake she glided there
Till, on his breast, a kiss-deep was her hair
That twisted serpent-wise in gold-red pain
From where his lips held high their proud disdain.
"Here, here," she whispered low, "here on my mouth
The swallow, Love, hath found his haunted South."

Then Dermid stooped and passionlessly kissed.
But therewith Grainne won what she had missed,
And that night was to her, and all sweet nights
Thereafter, as Love's flaming swallow-flights
Of passionate passion beyond speech to tell.
But Dermid knew how vain was any spell
Against the wrath of Finn: and Grainne's breath
To him was ever chill with Grainne's death;
Full well he knew that in a soundless place

His own wraith stood and with a moon-white face
Watched its own shadow laugh and shake its spear
Far in a phantom dell against a phantom deer.

THE SONG OF FIONULA

SLEEP, sleep, brothers dear, sleep and dream,
Nothing so sweet lies hid in all your years.
    Life is a storm-swept gleam
    In a rain of tears:
Why wake to a bitter hour, to sigh, to weep?
   How better far to sleep—
    To sleep and dream.

To sleep and dream, ah, that is well indeed:
  Better than sighs, better than tears,
Ye can have nothing better for your meed
       In all the years.
Why wake to a bitter hour, to sigh, to weep?
      How better far to sleep—
To sleep and dream, ah, that is well indeed!

DIM FACE OF BEAUTY

DIM face of Beauty haunting all the world,
Fair face of Beauty all too fair to see,
Where the lost stars adown the heavens are hurled
     There, there alone for thee
     May white peace be.

For here where all the dreams of men are whirled
Like sere torn leaves of autumn to and fro,
There is no place for thee in all the world,
    Who driftest as a star,
    Beyond, afar.

Beauty, sad face of Beauty, Mystery, Wonder,
What are these dreams to foolish babbling men
Who cry with little noises 'neath the thunder
        Of ages ground to sand,
        To a little sand.

The Mourners

(FROM THE BRETON)

WHEN they had made the cradle
    Of ivory and of gold,
Their hearts were heavy still
    With the sorrow of old.

And ever as they rocked, the tears
    Ran down, sad tears:
Who is it lieth dead therein,
    Dead all these weary years?

And still they rock that cradle there
    Of ivory and of gold:
For in their minds the shadow is
    The Shadow of Old.

They weep, and know not what they weep;
    They wait a vain re-birth:
Vanity of vanities, alas,
      For there is but one birth
      On the wide green earth.

DEAD LOVE

FROM THE GAELIC

(Heard sung by an old woman of the Island of Tires.)

IT is the grey rock I am,
And the grey rain on the rock:
It is the grey wave . . .
That grey hound.

What (is it) to be old:
(It is to be as) the grey moss in winter:
Alasdair-mo-ghaol,
It is long since my laughter.

Alasdair-mo-ghaol,
The breast is shrivelled
That you said was white
As canna in the wind.

THE RUNE OF AGE

O THOU that on the hills and wastes of Night a Shepherd,
Whose folds are flameless moons and icy planets,
Whose darkling way is gloomed with ancient sorrows:
Whose breath lies white as snow upon the olden,
Whose sigh it is that furrows breasts grown milkless,
Whose weariness is in the loins of man
And is the barren stillness of the woman:
O thou whom all would flee, and all must meet,
Thou that the Shadow art of Youth Eternal,
The gloom that is the hush'd air of the Grave,
The sigh that is between last parted love,
The light for aye withdrawing from weary eyes,
The tide from stricken hearts forever ebbing!

O thou the Elder Brother whom none loveth,
Whom all men hail with reverence or mocking,
Who broodest on the brows of frozen summits
Yet dreamest in the eyes of babes and children:
Thou, Shadow of the Heart, the Mind, the Life,
Who art that dusk What-is that is already Has-Been,
To thee this rune of the fathers to the sons
And of the sons to the sons, and mothers to new mothers—
To thee who art Aois,
To thee who art Age!

Breathe thy frosty breath upon my hair, for I am weary!
Lay thy frozen hand upon my bones that they support not,
Put thy chill upon the blood that it sustain not;
Place the crown of thy fulfilling on my forehead;
Throw the silence of thy spirit on my spirit;
Lay the balm and benediction of thy mercy
On the brain-throb and the heart-pulse and the life-spring—
For thy child that bows his head is weary,
For thy child that bows his head is weary.
I the shadow am that seeks the Darkness.
Age, that hath the face of Night unstarr'd and moonless,
Age, that doth extinguish star and planet,
Moon and sun and all the fiery worlds,
Give me now thy darkness and thy silence!

LEAVES, SHADOWS, AND DREAMS

I HAVE seen all things pass and all men go
Under the shadow of the drifting leaf:
   Green leaf, red leaf, brown leaf,
   Grey leaf blown to and fro,
     Blown to and fro.

I have seen happy dreams rise up and pass
Silent and swift as shadows on the grass:

Grey shadows of old dreams,
Grey beauty of old dreams,
Grey shadows in the grass.

THE VOICE AMONG THE DUNES

I HEAR the sea-wind sighing
    Where the dune-grasses grow,
The sighing of the dying
    Where the salt tides flow.

For where the salt tides flow
    The sullen dead are lifting
Tired arms, and to and fro
    Are idly drifting.

So through the grey dune-grasses
    Not the wind only cries,
But a dim sea-wrought Shadow
    Breathes drownëd sighs.

THE VEILED AVENGER

FRAGMENT OF A DRAMA

A Voice

. . . I am He,
The Veiled Avenger. I am clothed with shadow,
The silence and the shadow of your soul
Where it has withered slowly from the light.

Unseen Chorus

The Veiled Avenger speaks. He knows him not.

The Man

I hear a honey voice that murmureth peace,
Peace and oblivion. O ye secret doves
That feed the mind with sweet and perilous breaths
And murmur ever among gossamer dreams,
Bring me the tidings out of the hidden place
Wherein your wings wake fire. Come once again, wild
    doves
Of Beauty and Desire and the Twin Flame!
Wild doves, wild doves, bear unto me the flame
That rises moonwhite amid scarlet fire. . . .
                         (A lapwing wails.)
O melancholy bird, Dalua's messenger!
I am too weary now for further thought.

The Veiled Avenger

Pillows of sleepless sorrow. . . . Bow your head.
To-night I shall build up for you a place
Where sleep shall not be silent and where dreams
Shall whisper, and a little infinite voice
Shall wail as a wailing plover in your ears.
Then you shall know that shaken voice, and wake,
Crying your own name.

The Man

        Again, the wheeling cry
Where in the dusk the lapwing slips and falls
From ledge to ledge of darkness.

Unseen Chorus

        He knoweth not
His own bitter infinite cry we hear him cry!

The Three Evils of the Night

IN the great darkness where the shimmering stars
Are as the dazzle on the herring wave
Moveth the shadow of the end of wars:
But nightly comes as from a bloody grave
The Red Swineherd, who has no other name,
But who is grand and terrible, a flame
Fed upon blood and perishing lives and tears:
His feet are heavy with the bewildering years
Trodden dim bygone ages; and his eyes
Are vast and empty as the midnight skies.

Beware of the White Hound whose baying none hears
Although it is the wind that shakes the stars:
It is the Hound men saw in ancient wars:
It is the Hound that hunts the stricken years:
Pale souls in the ultimate silence see it gleam
Like a long lance o' the moon: it comes as a beam—
The soul is as blown dust within the wood
Wherein the White Hound moves and shadows brood.

Heed too the Flock of Birds from twilight places,
And from the desolate ways of ancient wars
Bewildered, terrible, and winged faces
Of souls adrift under the drifting stars:
But this I surely know, that the Red Flame
And the White Hound and the Dark Flock of Birds
Appal me no more, who never never again
Through rise and set and set and rise of pain
Shall hear the lips of her I loved whispering words
Or her hair cloud my lips moaning her name.

The Burthen of the Tide

THE tide was dark an' heavy with the burden that it bore,
I heard it talkin', whisperin', upon the weedy shore:
Each wave that stirred the sea-weed was like a closing door,
'Tis closing doors they hear at last who hear no more, no more,
                My Grief,
                No more!

The tide was in the salt sea-weed, and like a knife it tore,
The hoarse sea-wind went moaning, sooing, moaning o'er and o'er,
The wild sea-heart was brooding deep upon its ancient lore,
I heard the sob, the sooing sob, the dying sob at its core,
                My Grief,
                Its core!

The white sea-waves were wan and grey its ashy lips before;
The whirled spume between its jaws in floods did seaward pour—
O whisperin' weed, O wild sea-waves, O hollow baffled roar,
Since one thou hast, O dark dim Sea, why callest thou for more,
                My Grief,
                For more.

The Bells of Sorrow

IT is not only when the sea is dark and chill and desolate
I hear the singing of the queen who lives beneath the ocean:
Oft have I heard her chanting voice when noon swings wide his golden gate,
Or when the moonshine fills the wave with snowwhite mazy motion.

And some day will it hap to me, when the black waves are leaping,
Or when within the breathless green I see her shell-strewn door,
The fatal bells will lure me where my sea-drown'd death lies sleeping
Beneath the slow white hands of her who rules the sunken shore.

For in my heart I hear the bells that ring their fatal beauty,
The wild, remote, uncertain bells that chant their dim to-morrow:
The lonely bells of sorrow, the bells of fatal beauty,
From lonely heights within my heart tolling their lonely sorrow.

MIANN

MIANN ghaol, Sonas:
Miann bhithe, Sith:
Miann anama, Flathas:
Miann Dhe ... gile rùn Gu bhrath.

DESIRES

THE Desire of Love, Joy:
The Desire of Life, Peace:
The Desire of the Soul, Heaven:
The Desire of God ... a flamewhite secret for ever.

* * *

Gleidh sinn a glinn nan diar
'Us a taigh nan diamha dubhra.

Keep us from the Glen of Tears
And from the House of Sorrow.

www.ingramcontent.com/pod-product-compliance
Lightning Source LLC
Chambersburg PA
CBHW020430010526
44118CB00010B/506